AF441587

The Daily Life of a Roman Family in the Ancient Times

Ancient History Books for Kids

Children's Ancient History

BABY PROFESSOR

EDUCATION KIDS

Speedy Publishing LLC

40 E. Main St. #1156

Newark, DE 19711

www.speedypublishing.com

Copyright 2017

All Rights reserved. No part of this book may be reproduced or used in any way or form or by any means whether electronic or mechanical, this means that you cannot record or photocopy any material ideas or tips that are provided in this book

For about a thousand years, the Roman Republic, followed by the Roman Empire, was a huge force in history. We think of Roman legions marching and fighting, and senators making speeches, and how good or bad different emperors were.

But what about everyday life?

How did an average Roman family live each day?

Let's find out!

Throughout the empire, the most exciting places to live were the cities. Whether it was Rome itself, or a new city in a new province, there was a mix of cultures and peoples, of opportunities and challenges. The population of Rome included not just native Romans or people from other parts of Italy, but Spaniards, Syrians, Britons, North Africans, Greeks, Gauls, and Jews.

People moved to the cities to make a better life for themselves, and to have more choices about how they lived. In the country, you worked as a servant of your crops and animals, and there were few options for recreation or leisure.

Ancient Roman House

Roman Forum

A lot of city-dwellers lived in poverty, struggling to find the job that would let them afford a better way of life. A lot of what we now think of as careers, like teaching, medicine, and accounting, were largely done by slaves, not citizens. This cut down on the ways people could make a living.

If you were well-off in a Roman city, you lived in a villa. Villas tended to show blank walls to the street to protect the goods and life inside. Within there would be gardens and unroofed spaces open to the sky, and a rooms for entertaining, food preparation and consumption, sleeping, and work. Villas were the mansions of the rich and powerful.

Roman Villa

Roman bath ruins

If you were not rich, but not poor, you might live in a domus. The front of your home might be a shop facing the street, where you sold and repaired shoes or did the other work that earned your living. Behind your shop would be the atrium, the public area where you entertained visitors. In the middle of the atrium was a pool that had no roof above it. The pool was not just decorative: it collected rainwater that fell through the roof opening, and the water was used for cleaning and cooking. There would probably be a shrine in one corner of the atrium where you honored household gods. To the sides of the atrium were rooms used as bedrooms, offices, storerooms and shops.

If you were poor, as most people were, you had living space in one of the apartment blocks called insulae, or "islands". The government made no effort to provide housing for the poor, and took little care to make sure the insulae were well-built so they did not suddenly fall down.

Roman Apartment

Apartments in the lower floors of insulae could be fairly comfortable, with many of the comforts of a domus. However, the poorer you were, the higher up in insulae you lived. You had little access to fresh water or natural light, and perhaps the whole family would have to share a single room. In the higher floors of insulae, you paid your rent by the day or week and the landlord could throw you out at any time. And, of course, the building could just fall down around you.

For all Romans, rich or poor, the family was the most important unit in society. In theory, the father, the paterfamilias, was all-powerful. He had the power of life and death over slaves, and could even sell his children into slavery.

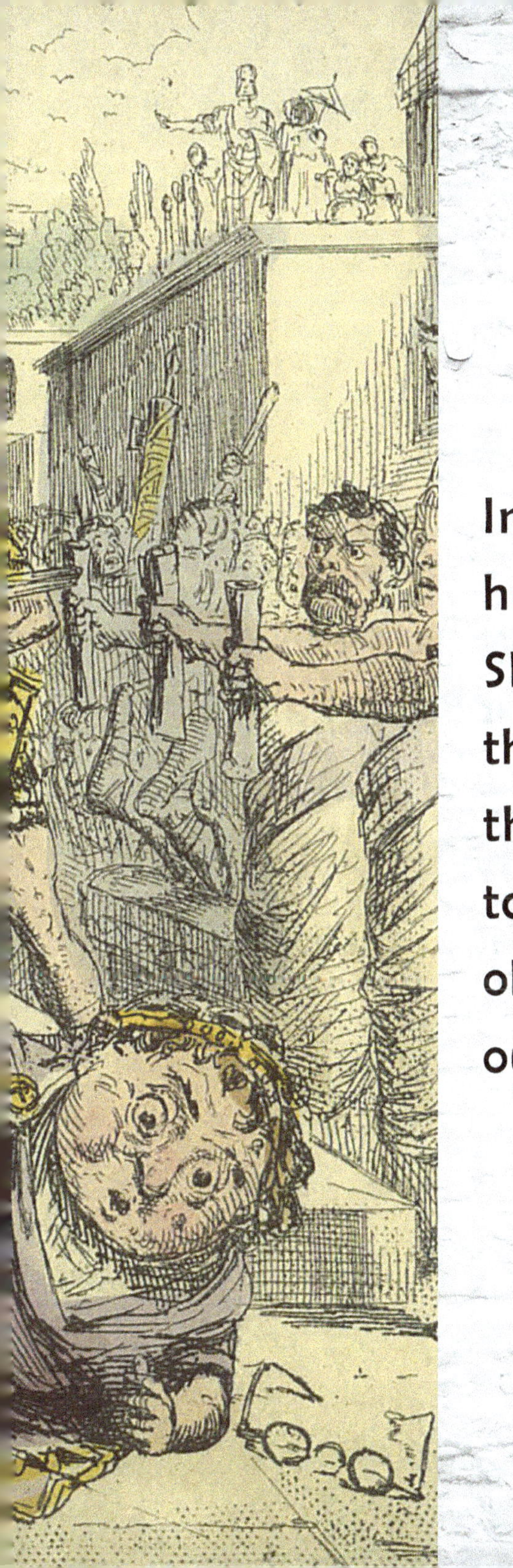

In practice, however, the mother had great power and influence. She ran the household, managed the slaves and servants, made sure the accounts were balanced, and taught the children until they were old enough for a tutor or to be sent out as apprentices.

Under the Republic, women's rights in public, and how they could even appear in public, were quite limited. As the Empire evolved, women's rights improved somewhat, and it could be they who ran the bakery or pharmacy in the front of the domus.

FOOD

The main meal of the day was in the late afternoon. Breakfast and lunch might be mainly bread or porridge, with some cheese on the side.

What you got to eat for the main meal of the day depended, of course, on whether you were rich or poor. Poor families saw very little meat and lived mainly on grains and boiled vegetables. Many of the poor were malnourished and suffered poor health. The government provided a monthly grain allowance to families to keep people from actually dying of hunger in the streets.

For wealthier families, the menu was more varied and more nutritious. There would be eels, fish, oysters, pheasants and chickens, and a wide variety of carefully-prepared fruits and vegetables in rich sauces. Ice brought down from the mountains would allow for chilled food in hot weather.

A lot of the ingredients we think of as part of an Italian meal, like tomatoes and pasta, did not exist yet in Europe. Tomatoes came from the New World and pasta from China, but both arrived in Italy long after the Empire had collapsed.

No matter what the recipe, most Romans would throw in some "garum" (fermented fish sauce) to improve the dish, whether it was meat or millet or pears in honey. The making, importing, and selling of garum was a major part of the Roman economy, and may have been the main reason for some of Rome's military conquests.

People drank wine, mixed with water according to taste. For the poor, there were public fountains where they could get water at no cost.

Fontana di Trevi Fountain

THE WORK DAY

People got up very early in the morning, and conducted almost all business before the heat of the middle of the day. Houses did not have any way to refrigerate food, so for most families somebody had to go to the market every day to buy food. People who lived in villas usually had farms in the country, so every day slaves would deliver food from the farms.

Shops opened before dawn and closed by noon. Sometimes some shops opened again at the end of the afternoon. The law courts, libraries, and political offices worked on the same schedule. The poor, of course, worked a much longer day for much lower wages, and had no choice about taking time off.

Roman Bath

If the morning was for work, the afternoons were for entertainments and leisure activities. Rich and poor alike went to the baths, huge structures with washing facilities and great, shallow swimming pools where people could lounge around and socialize. Different pools were kept at different temperatures, from very hot to relatively cold. There were also running tracks, gyms for exercise, and meeting rooms where people could argue politics or make business deals.

Beside the baths, people could go to the great outdoor theaters to see comedies and tragedies by both Roman and Greek playwrights, and huge spectacles involving massed singers, trained animals, and acrobats. Plays had to take place during the day because there was no way to provide enough lighting in those days for a big indoor theater.

Roman Ampitheater

Colosseum

At the Coliseum or other sports venues, people could watch, and bet on, chariot races, gladiators fighting each other, boxing matches, and other diversions. There were no team sports as we have them now.

The government took seriously the need to provide entertainment, along with the grain supply, for the whole population. The theory was that if people got enough "bread and circuses" (The Circus Maximus was not a performing circus with clowns and trick riders, but a race track), they would be more content even if their lives were quite hard.

At the end of a relaxing afternoon, people would go home for the main meal of the day with their family. They would go to bed early to get ready for the start of the new day.

LEARNING

Mothers were the teachers when the children were small. As children grew older, families who could afford them hired tutors or bought educated slaves who would teach the family children. Teachers were often quite strict, and had permission to beat their students if the students were not paying attention.

PYTHAGORAS
PAR   IMPAR
1 2 3 4 5 6 7 8 9 . 10 11 12
4913   37995
2367   27
7480   264965
             75990
          1025865
968
3257
3771

Students learned basic arithmetic, which was quite tricky, as the Romans used groups of letters to indicate numbers. The sequence 13, 14, 15 would be XIII, XIV, XV to a Roman. Romans had no symbol for zero until late in the Empire.

Romans also learned public speaking, history, weights and measures, reading and writing, and philosophy. Romans of higher-class families learned Greek as well as Latin, as Greek philosphers, historians, and playwrights had produced so much important material.

Q MARCIO QVI
MAXIMO OB MVNIFI
CENTIAM Q MARCI STA
PICIS ILELIVS FICB
EIVS MERITA EXCVSET
CIVIBAS THVGGENSIS
POST MORTEM DD PP
CVR IICARIBVS G MODIO
IVSTIO FNVMARIO HONORIN

RELIGION

There were temples all through Roman cities, with daily rituals and offerings to please the many gods. At home, people had shrines for their household gods and gods they honored especially. The paterfamilias of the household would lead prayers for the family and bless the children (or not bless them, if they had been bad!), and there were many religious holidays all year round.

In many ways, people long ago lived and thought just as we do now. In other ways they were quite different. Read other Baby Professor books to learn more about the people of our past.

Visit
BABY PROFESSOR
EDUCATION KIDS
www.BabyProfessorBooks.com
to download Free Baby Professor eBooks
and view our catalog of new and exciting
Children's Books

www.ingramcontent.com/pod-product-compliance
Lightning Source LLC
Chambersburg PA
CBHW080745180726
48003CB00021B/2889